EFFECTIVE
APPRAISAL SKI

CW00722244

Graham Taylor

60 Minutes Success Skills Series

Copyright © David Grant Publishing Limited 1998

First published 1998 by
David Grant Publishing Limited
80 Ridgeway
Pembury
Kent TN2 4EZ
United Kingdom

99 98 97 10 9 8 7 6 5 4 3 2 1

60 Minutes Success Skills Series is an imprint of
David Grant Publishing Limited

British Library Cataloguing in Publication Data
A CIP catalogue record for this book is available from the British Library

ISBN 1-901306-07-0

Cover design: Steve Haynes
Text design: Graham Rich
Production editor: Paul Stringer

Typeset in Futura by
Archetype IT Ltd, web site http://www.archetype-it.com
Printed and bound in Great Britain by
T.J. International Ltd, Padstow, Cornwall

This book is printed on acid-free paper

All names mentioned in the text have been changed to protect the identity
of the business people involved. Any resemblance to existing companies or
people is entirely coincidental.

CONTENTS

ABOUT *EFFECTIVE APPRAISAL SKILLS*

Can you learn how to appraise successfully in just one hour? The answer is a resounding "Yes!"

The only bit of waffle in this book

The 60 Minutes Success Skills Series is for people with neither the time nor the patience to trawl through acres of jargon. If you want to avoid management-speak and page-filling waffle, this book is definitely for you.

Like all books in the series, *Effective Appraisal Skills* has been written in the belief that you can learn all you really need to know quickly and without fuss The aim is to provide essential, practical advice that you can use straight away.

Is this book for you?

Most companies, whatever their size, use some system of formal appraisals. Very often, these are treated like annual events that have to be endured, like a full medical examination.

This book is for you if:

○ *You can't really see the point of formal appraisals and . . .*
○ *. . . nor can those around you, especially your staff;*
○ *You want to communicate better with your staff but don't know where to start;*
○ *You struggle to deal with issues of discipline;*
○ *You are never sure that you are giving enough praise;*
○ *You spend most of your management time fighting fires.*

By investing just one hour of your time in reading *Effective Appraisal Skills*, you can learn quickly how to make appraisals an integral part of your management style. You will find out how to:

○ *Create an appraisal process that works every time;*
○ *Make appraisals on-going and constructive;*
○ *Plan and prepare properly;*
○ *Interview perfectly;*
○ *Follow up productively;*
○ *Use appraisals to get the best from people and become more effective yourself.*

This book takes a very different approach to the question of appraisals from most others. It does not simply re-hash current theory but, rather, sets a bold and exciting challenge to you the reader to re-think your attitude to appraisals as a whole. If you want a book that tells you how to fill the forms out sufficiently well to take the heat off until next year, don't bother reading this one. However, if you want to learn to appraise on a daily basis and thereby become a superb manager of people, read on!

How to use this book

The message in this book is "It's OK to skim". You don't have to read it all at once, or follow every tip to the letter. *Effective Appraisal Skills* has been written to dip into, so feel free to flick through to find the help you most need.

You also do not have to do everything advised straight away. This book is a collection of hands-on tips designed to help you build the foundations of an appraisals process which will allow you to boost morale, build up people's skills and effectiveness, and, at the same time, become a much better manager.

You will find that there are some graphic features used throughout the book:

This means "Something for you to think about" – it sets the scene and identifies the problems by prompting you to think about situations which should instantly feel familiar.

With the problems diagnosed, these features give you the framework for an action plan – this will help you to get your own ideas in order.

This feature appears at the end of each chapter. It is a check-list which condenses all of the advice given throughout the chapter. Similar features appear within chapters which are overflowing with ideas!

WELCOME

As you read through the chapters, you will come across lots of tips and practical advice on how to appraise people well. You can start by going straight to any of the graphic features, which will ask you to either think about a problem or to do something about it and give you some ideas as to how best to tackle it. If you're really pushed for time, you can always go direct to the tips features at the end of each chapter.

The chapter summaries are also a useful reminder when you come to look at this book in the future.

Good luck!

What's in this chapter for you

> *The all too common reality*
> *Back to basics*
> *Keep it regular*
> *The manager's role*
> *Where appraisals go wrong*
> *What appraisals should be*

The all too common reality

> ❝ *I dread it – the annual round of filling out pointless forms, asking the staff stupid questions and then getting them to fill out their own self-assessment forms. Frankly, it's like a cross between a school report and a job interview. Once it's all done, they get filed only to be taken out and looked at the same time next year. I've got better things to be doing with my time.* ❞
> **– Richard Cross, team leader**

Does Richard's negative attitude strike a chord with you? Does the formal act of appraising your staff – or of being appraised yourself – seem to be a total waste of time to everyone in your organisation except the personnel director?

The simple fact is that in most organisations the act of appraisal has become institutionalised and, as an instrument of the institution, has been applied unthinkingly and without understanding.

> ❝ *We have a formal appraisal twice a year. The boss seems duty bound to find fault so he picks you up on little things. If he has a problem with my work, why can't he tell me as I'm doing it? I always come out of the appraisal feeling completely demoralised – surely, that's not the point!* ❞
> **– Kerry Bridges, customer service clerk**

Appraisals can and should be one of the most effective and important management tools. Used correctly, appraisals will help you to get the most out of individuals and the teams that they constitute. However, if used incorrectly, you can end up with a demotivated work force which will prove impossible to manage properly.

> Is the appraisal system you use a help or hindrance to your ability as a manager? Is it something that you just have to put up with, like the Spice Girls?
> What about your staff? Are they enriched by the appraisal system, or bored rigid by it?

Back to Basics

The great thing about appraisals is that there is nothing mystical, magical or indeed difficult about the process. Most of it is pure common sense, but you have to understand the reason for them in the first place and a little of the theory.

Let's start with a definition.

Appraisal is the on-going, two-way communication process which assesses and reviews

○ *capabilities,*
○ *performance, and*
○ *needs.*

It provides a means of giving and getting **regular** feedback.

Put simply, appraisal involves letting people know what is required and expected of them, assessing how they are doing, reviewing this with them regularly and agreeing with them what happens next.

We will look in detail in future chapters at mechanisms and methods of successful appraisal. However, the term "appraisal" refers throughout this book to the informal day-to-day skills of people management which link up to the formal systems which most companies have.

> Never forget that unless your appraisals are
>
> ❑ **on-going** and
> ❑ **two-way**
>
> then you are not doing your job as a manager properly.

No apologies – these messages will appear throughout this book at regular intervals. They are probably the most important things to remember throughout the entire process, but the ones which most people forget about.

Keep it regular

> How often do you undertake appraisal activities in a typical working week?
>   Unless you can reply "several times daily" the chances are you are not realising the full power of appraisal as a management tool.

Surprised? Most people equate the appraisal process with filling in forms and receiving terse memos from the personnel manager because these forms are a day late. The formal elements are important, but equally important in your role as a manger is to be appraising **all of the time**.

> ❝ *Every time my boss appraises me, I cannot help but agree with him that my main area of improvement needs to be in the appraising of my own staff! However, I just don't find the time to do it on a regular basis as I'm just too busy getting on with my own job.* ❞
> **– Steve Crane, accountant**

Steve's problem is a very common one – he is caught in the classic trap of being too busy to appraise others and yet overworked and stressed out because he isn't managing others through effective appraisal.

Appraisal provides a discipline to enable people to manage successfully. If done properly, it will force you as a manager to think about your staff and what they are doing. Without it, you will constantly be fire-fighting and reacting – your job will be controlling you, not the other way around, as it should be.

The manager's role

Don't worry, we're not heading off into pages of heavy management theory! However, whether you have one or a thousand and one people reporting to you, you do need to think what your role as a manager demands of you.

Traditionally, the role of the manager has been seen in purely functional terms – good management involves planning, organising, controlling, motivating and evaluating. All of these things are obviously important, but do not fully reflect the changing role of the manager. A better way of looking at management is to say that:

> ❝ *A manager should develop and support the environment for success.* ❞

Now, to do this well, you conscientiously need to commit time to working with those around you, both individually and in groups, in order to help them develop the skills to perform their tasks well. This involves a range of *developmental* skills which include, coaching, problem solving, counselling, team working and delegating, as well as appraising.

Management is changing throughout the world and it is through heightened developmental skills that you and those around you will achieve success. Effective appraisal is central to this.

Where appraisals go wrong

We've all heard horror stories – and you'll read several in this book – about people being sacked on the spot in an appraisal, or reduced to tears over alleged wrongdoings. Unfortunately, extreme behaviour and simple bad practice have tarnished the image of the appraisal.

Consequently, people can view appraisals as a waste of time and effort when the real problem is more likely to be that the manager concerned is a waste of space!

See if you recognise some or all of the following scenarios.

Reactive or immediate appraisal

> ❝ *Every time something goes wrong, our manager screams at somebody for the next hour and reduces us all to gibbering wrecks. We all work on the principle that if the manager is not hyperventilating, then we are doing a good job!* ❞
> – **Greg Campbell, telesales executive**

One-way appraisal

❝ *My manager is great at telling me what to do, when and how to do it, but she never listens to what I think and the problems I have. It is **so** frustrating dealing with her!* ❞
– Marie Rooney, graphic designer

Negative appraisal

❝ *I'm always being told what I am doing wrong, what my faults are, and how bad my attitude is. It turns out the supervisor says the same to everyone. I think he is so insecure about his own position that he doesn't want to encourage any of us to do too well in case it shows him in his true light.* ❞
– Nicola Rainer, fashion designer.

Irregular appraisal

❝ *Once a year, the supervisor fills in the forms, then drags you into the office to tell you all the things you have or have not done over the year. Your only role is to nod in the right places, and look apologetic or ecstatic depending on what sort of a mood she's in. You then keep your head down until next year.* ❞
– Rod Fine, lab technician

Blame allocation

❝ *When something goes wrong, management immediately want to find somebody to blame . They love post-mortems, but don't seem to be able to learn anything from them! The same problems keep occurring and in the end you avoid using your initiative over anything in case you get the blame.* ❞
– Jim Byrne, boiler operative

Limited follow-up

❝ *We spend a huge amount of time reviewing how we are doing and go through all the stages of the formal appraisal. However, once the forms are signed and sent to personnel, nothing happens. None of the commitments made by either party is stuck to.* ❞
– Nial Reynolds, bookseller

Confrontation appraisal

"The boss is always aggressive. Even his body language screams at you. And when he wags his finger in your face and shouts at you, he looks such an idiot. Someone will thump him one day!"
– Steph Thurlow, catering manager

Do these experiences ring any bells with you? Be honest!

These classic mistakes are made in companies world-wide during appraisals. You will have recognised many of the attitudes expressed and perhaps even have been shamed by some! By looking at such negative responses it becomes easier to identify the key features of good appraisals.

What appraisals should be

Ask any manager who has mastered the the appraisals process and they'll tell you that it's the most potent managerial skill.

Effective appraisals begin with an understanding of their true worth.

1. Appraisals are not an annual exercise in generating additional paperwork. Think of the appraisal as a creative tool which enables you to manage better.
2. By using appraisal skills properly, you will be letting people know what they are doing well and where improvements need to be made.
3. Through appraising you will be able to identify problem areas early on and act promptly to overcome them. Your team or department should then run like a well-oiled machine!
4. Ensure you make your appraisals genuinely on-going and two way.
5. Don't restrict yourself to appraising your staff only at certain times – start when you get to work and stop when you get home!

What's in this chapter for you

The five point appraisal blueprint
Step 1: Benchmarking
Step 2: Assessment
Step 3: Reviewing
Step 4: Agreeing what's next
Step 5: Follow-up

We've seen that appraisal is an important management tool and that getting it wrong can have a damaging effect on all those involved. Appraisal is vital if you and your staff want to thrive. We will now look at how to start doing it properly, and the benefits this will have for everyone.

> ❝ *After our department was formed, we were sure our new boss was omnipresent, but it wasn't a case of Big Brother. She was just always there to explain clearly what needed to be done and show us how to solve problems for ourselves.* ❞
> **– Sophie O'Riorden, distribution clerk**

By now you should fully understand that the appraisal process is not simply something you do at the behest of the personnel department. It is as an on-going and constant activity (as I think we may have mentioned before!) which will help you to get the best out of your people and improve your own efficiency.

> ❝ *The team runs like clockwork now and the boss has disappeared on a six month fact-finding mission to the Seychelles.* ❞
> **– Sophie O'Riorden**

Imagine in this chapter that you have a new member of staff – let's call him Chris – starting in your department. You have two choices. The first is the "chuck him in at the deep end" approach, very often followed up by the "hang him high" manoeuvre when it all goes horribly wrong.

The second approach, which you should follow if you have any serious intention of having a long and prosperous management career, is to work with Chris from day one, to lay out clearly what is expected, and to check continuously the progress being made. In other words, start the appraisal process immediately.

Let's look at this process in detail and follow your dealings with Chris in his first (and, hopefully, happy) year in your department.

The Five Point Appraisal Blueprint

There are five key steps to establishing an effective appraisal process for Chris from day one. Let's look at each one in turn.

Step 1: Benchmarking

Your first task is to explicitly set out to Chris what is expected in his new role, and then to communicate that clearly. Chris should then know what precisely he is supposed to be doing and how his success will be measured.

These criteria are called *benchmarks*. Put simply, a benchmark gives a standard against which performance can be judged.

> **❝** *I walked out of my last job following an appraisal. The manager accused me of not doing various jobs very well. I hadn't even been aware I was meant to be doing them in the first place!* **❞**
> **– Trudi Mackenzie, clerical assistant**

In order to make sure Chris does not go the way of Trudi, you need to make your requirements and expectations clear and ensure that they are understood – you also need to remain consistent in these expectations.

Your benchmarks can be set out to Chris in a number of ways – the following are the most common. Choose whichever is most appropriate for your particular circumstances.

Job description

This can prove a useful starting point, but on its own may be too general and vague. Very often a job description:

○ *does not detail precise day-to-day activity, and*
○ *is not looked at regularly.*

(It is also highly likely that you gave Chris his job description on the morning he started so he's made no contribution to it!)

Accountability statement

This is a summary of key areas/aspects that the jobholder will be accountable for. For example if Chris is employed in stock control, then one of his accountabilities could be "the value of the total stock". Accountability statements can be very useful as they obviously state requirements and can be put together with a high degree of consultation.

Standards of performance

This is a statement of what is required in the key aspects of the job and more general disciplinary issues. Some examples may be:

- ○ *"All customer enquiries will be formally acknowledged within three working hours."*
- ○ *"All staff meeting customers face-to-face will wear the designated uniform and name badge."*
- ○ *"Staff must be in at 9.00 a.m. and must not leave until 5.30 p.m. without permission."*

It should be possible to break Chris's role down into key standards of performance which will help to focus his attention on what is important. If well phrased and clear, they can be used as the basis for assessing individual and team performance. To do this, however, you need to monitor and measure the attainment of standards constantly.

> **Avoid vagueness when compiling standards of performance. "All staff must try really hard and do a good job" might prove to be somewhat open to interpretation!**

Objectives

These are targets which should help to move Chris forward and set out the changes or improvements required. Remember, objectives need always to be SMART:

- ○ *Specific*
- ○ *Measurable*
- ○ *Achievable*

○ *Realistic*
○ *Timebound.*

Objectives should provide a way of agreeing and focusing attention on what is important over the next time period.

> Always set and communicate your requirements and expectations explicitly and visibly. Be SMART!

> **❝** *There was an unwritten rule that if you only took half an hour for lunch, you could leave a bit earlier in the evening without having to ask permission. It had been going on for years, and no one said any different until the new boss came in. In my first appraisal with her, she criticised me for my time keeping, which I felt was totally unjustified.* **❞**
> **– Rachel Collins, housing manager**

In most companies, there will be informal rules as to what is acceptable behaviour. These can almost become traditions. If you are not formal and explicit with Chris at the earliest possible stage about what you expect from him, he may well pick up bad habits from those around him, thinking his behaviour is perfectly acceptable. Given that management and staff expectations often differ, conflict can arise purely because you have not been clear about what it is you want and expect.

> When you are thinking about your requirements and expectations, get input from those who will be most affected by them – your staff. Consult and involve them at all stages and you will make them feel that they have a stake in what has been agreed.

Step 2: Assessment

Having set out your explicit requirements and expectations to Chris, you've now got to find out whether these are being met. The way to do this is by assessing him as he is going about his daily work. However, that does not mean sitting there with a pen and paper studying him constantly and making notes!

> Find time frequently to review what your staff are doing and how they are performing. Don't be obstructive when you are doing this but fit it in to your every day management style – it's all about visible and supportive management!

You cannot make an assessment instantly – it has got to be done over time in order to get a true overall impression of a situation. Too often assessment, and therefore appraisal, is unfairly coloured by one high profile incident rather than a considered and balanced view point.

> ❝ *The only time I forgot to use the protective cover over the cutter, the boss was there! I know I was wrong, but it hasn't happened since and won't happen again. But he just refuses to forget about it and still mentions the incident three years on!* ❞
> **– George Reynolds, die cutter**

You must ensure that you are always assessing Chris against your requirements and expectations. This assessment must be based upon visible outcomes and behaviour rather than opinions and intuitions which may have been formed inaccurately because of one untypical event.

Be very aware that you are assessing Chris over the coming months and comparing his actions against agreed consistent benchmarks.

> Be consistent! Don't change the rules half-way through. You've outlined your requirement and expectations in consultation with your staff – stick to them!

Step 3: Reviewing

❝ *The first review my boss gave me was awful. He simply called me into the office without any warning at all, sat me down and told me*

*that if I did not get on top of our overseas debtors, I'd be looking for
another job. He didn't even give me the chance to remind him that
I'd only been in the job for three months and that the system I'd
inherited was worse than useless. I got another job soon after that.* "
– Carolyn Stafford, credit controller

The review is central to the appraisal process. It provides the
opportunity for an open, two-way discussion with an individual
which will give valuable information about their progress. You
should undertake to do this with Chris within a matter of weeks of
his starting and then regularly from there on.

> **Make sure that the review is conducted face-to-face with the
> person concerned and that it provides a genuine opportunity for
> an exchange of views. What you are going to say must be well
> thought out in advance – and give Chris plenty of warning so
> that he too can be prepared.**

The review discussion is your opportunity to instigate change and
improvement as well as to reinforce positive behaviour and to
praise success. Equally importantly, it is your opportunity to get
direct input and involvement from Chris – by doing so you may
well find that he has his own solutions to problems that have
given you cause for concern. By using and encouraging his input,
reviews (and, therefore, appraisals) become easier and more
effective – and Chris will feel valued and important.

> **Never be tempted to make the instant review. By doing so you
> may be reacting purely to an untypical snap shot of behaviour.
> Instant reviews based on instant assessments very often lead to
> unnecessary conflict and confrontation.**

Step 4: Agreeing what comes next

" *We have regular appraisals at which various problems are
discussed. However, that's it – all we do is discuss them. The boss*

never puts forward suggestions as to what to do about them and I have stopped bothering as no one listens to my ideas. 99
– Dave Greenhead, department supervisor

There need to be outcomes from your on-going appraisal activities and these need to be explicit and easily understood. When you are dealing with issues as they arise with Chris, you need to ensure that he sees you taking decisions and action to move the situation and his development forward.

> **Make sure that you and the appraisee are now thinking about what will happen in the future rather than dwelling upon what has gone before.**

There are many different types of outcome which you could come up with at this stage. Here are some examples.

Perceived problem	Agreed outcome
Chris lacks self-confidence in dealing with customers	Internal customer care course, including assessed role playing
He is nearly ready for promotion but needs to increase his financial and commercial awareness	Chris to prepare a project business plan with guidance and support of manager and finance manager
Chris has a poor telephone manner	Telephone skills course resulting in an agreed personal improvement plan
He lacks knowledge and understanding of the quality management system	Structured coaching with experienced team member

By agreeing such outcomes with Chris, you will have mapped out the way forward – you have clearly and specifically agreed what is going to happen next and who is going to do what.

Step 5: Follow-up

To make the appraisal process credible and ultimately useful, you need to follow-up actions and activities and make sure that the things which were agreed upon actually happen. Chris will need to have faith that you really believe in the process.

> **Say what you are going to do, and do what you say.**

Any action you take needs to be obvious because your staff will pay attention as much to what you don't do as to what you do. They will judge the importance you place on their development and the appraisal system as a whole by how rigorously you follow through agreed action. If you are perceived to be simply going through the motions, Chris and his colleagues will lose respect both for you and for the whole appraisal system.

The time to start is now

You can now see how to close the loop on the appraisal system and are in a position start the process all over again. Your aim should be to appraise consistently and continuously.

If you get it right from the start, appraisals will give you a managerial edge.

1. Begin the appraisal process from day one.
2. Always set standards of performance against which people can be judged. These should always be clear and reasonable – don't leave room for misunderstanding!
3. Set objectives which are specific, measurable, achievable, realistic and timebound – be SMART!
4. Consult with your staff at all times about your requirements and expectations.
5. Never draw conclusions from one-off events.
6. Always agree outcomes so that everyone knows who is going to do what next.
7. Do what you say you are going to do. If you fail to keep to what you say, you will discredit yourself as a manager and the entire appraisal system.
8. Schedule agreed action, and ensure that you carry out your commitments on time.

What's in this chapter for you?

Make it happen all of the time
Don't be so formal!
Start as you mean to go on
Individual reviews
Team reviews
Team meetings
Carry on appraising

Make it happen all of the time

Before going any further, let's just remind ourselves about the underlying principles involved in successful appraisal. It is worth looking again at our definition from chapter 1 (just in case you suffer from short-term memory loss!)

Appraisal is the on-going, two-way communication process which assesses and reviews

○ *capabilities,*
○ *performance, and*
○ *needs.*

It provides a means of giving and getting regular feedback.

Appraisal is a long-term commitment and is central to how you manage and develop your staff. It is a philosophy which should underpin your entire approach to management. And, most important of all, appraisal should be taking place all of the time.
    In this chapter, you are going to learn the techniques to ensure you are appraising your staff 100% of the time.

Don't be so formal!

The starting point for effective on-going appraisal must be the temporary suspension of your belief in formal systems – whilst reading this chapter, forget all about the formal systems set down by the company you currently work with!
    Consider the case of George "the system" Sinclair.

❝ *My people have a clear understanding of how they are doing and what is expected of them. We have a very sophisticated appraisal system which allows for a detailed annual review, followed by a six-monthly update system. It is open and two-way and allows people to know exactly where they stand – I swear by it!* ❞
– George Sinclair, accounts manager

Formal systems are important but are simply organisational tools to help you to do your job well – they can never replace effective management.

Management systems are there for the benefit of your staff. Your staff are not there for the benefit of your management systems. Where do you stand on this notion?

❝ *My last boss was addicted to systems. If there wasn't a procedure then it didn't get done. My problem is that I'm ambitious and I needed regular feedback as to how I was getting on. If I asked him, he'd tell me that there was a another eight weeks, or whatever, to go to the next appraisal and we could discuss it then. The worst thing was that he would always have some criticism of me which he only ever told me at the formal appraisal. If he had told me when I asked I could have done something about it. He was systems mad – it makes you wonder what his home life is like!* ❞
– Charlie Green, ex-member of George Sinclair's team

We'll leave it to Charlie to ponder why George's fifth wife has joined the Foreign Legion.

The point here is that George relies completely on the system and has made himself totally inflexible in his day-to-day management. If a situation doesn't fit the system in George's world view, then it will have to wait.

Formal appraisal is a means to an end, not an end in itself. Don't fall into the trap of relying totally on the paperwork and formal interviews of your company's appraisal machine. It could leave you so distant from the **real** issues that you'll be left with unmanageable staff and an operation which any sane accountant would shut down.

Start as you mean to go on

" My new assistant had an appalling telephone manner, didn't like filing – nails excepted – and had a major attitude problem. I let it go for a couple of months because I was too busy to address the issue. I decided to tackle it at her formal quarterly review. By then, she thought that her behaviour was totally acceptable and couldn't understand why I was criticising her! "
– Karen Winter, recruitment agent

How is it that we never seem to find the time to deal with poor performance at the very start? We'd much rather pretend that it is one-off behaviour and will sort itself out, and that we are too busy to deal with it right now. The crazy thing is that the time and effort involved in sorting out a problem once it has escalated can be truly horrendous.

In Karen's case, she should have sat down with the new assistant early on and laid out what was expected. By relying on a formal appraisal system as a cure all, she was allowing unsatisfactory behaviour to escalate.

Good management is about preventing problems and avoiding crises. It is not about solving problems and dealing with crises. You must make time to appraise your staff on an on-going basis. Don't wait for the annual formalities – appraisal activities both formal and informal should be happening every day.

On-going appraisal should be a state of mind which means that a combination of formal and informal appraisal becomes an automatic way of managing people. The most effective people managers do not even have to think in terms of "appraising" because it comes so naturally to them.

" The best manager I ever worked for always had time for a chat and would poke her head round the office door to see if I was all right. She would let me know when things weren't happening in the way she wanted but always in a positive open manner. The formal

appraisals we had annually were really constructive and, believe it or not, enjoyable! 99
– George Carter, social worker

To master the art of on-going, informal appraisals, you will have to use most of the following methods.

Individual reviews

66 *Whenever I take on a new role I spend the first few days observing my new department. I try to be unobtrusive about it but also fairly methodical. If I don't commit to this, I find that months can go by in a busy blur without me getting to know my staff properly.* 99
– Ian Grant, divisional manager

If you are taking over a new team or establishing a new department, you won't know the individuals and they won't know you so you need to commit to Ian's approach and find time to understand what is going on.

You are trying to answer the following questions:

○ **How is the individual doing?**
. . . against performance standards and personal objectives.
○ **What does the individual need to perform more effectively?**
. . . perhaps training, coaching, encouragement, discipline, more money.
○ **What is the individual capable of in the future?**
. . . do they have the potential for new responsibilities, or a promotion?

You must assess your staff against the above criteria over time and in a balanced way. Avoid snap judgements. Build up a long-term picture of the person as an individual, within the team and in the organisation as a whole.

Team reviews

Appraising your people as a team is just as vital as individual reviews. Very often we forget to assess people's role within a team and at the same time forget the different dynamics which go on within the framework of the team.

❝ My boss hasn't yet grasped that we are all interdependent and that unless we work together everything will end in disaster. He doesn't seem to appreciate that part of our working as a team means there will be a certain amount of repartee and jokes flying around. He walked in on the second day, got us together and said there was too much noise and not enough work going on. ❞

– Mary Phillips, team co-ordinator

As with individual reviews, you should be trying to answer the following basic questions:

- ○ **How is the team performing?**
  . . . against objectives and standards of performance, and overall.
- ○ **How is the team functioning?**
  . . . what are the day-to-day operating methods; how efficient and effective is the team?
- ○ **Where is the team going?**
  . . . revised targets and objectives, long-term goals and linkage to the organisation as a whole.

By thinking about these questions, and getting answers to them on a day-to-day basis, you will be mapping out the team's position and providing the basis for communicating to the team how they are doing and where they are going.

"Ten-minute chats"

So, you've observed your people and undertaken your individual reviews – what now?

❝ It turns out that what my boss had been doing was compiling dossiers on us all. He then sprung these on us at the annual review. It was like living in a police state! ❞

– Irma Hawkes, supervisor

What you don't do is store it all up like Irma's boss!

Schedule in your diary regular ten-minute chunks of time. Use these to sit down with your people on a one-to-one basis and discuss progress informally.

People like to know how they are doing and that you as their boss are concerned about their progress and aware of what is going on. Brief, informal conversations are a perfect way to keep communicating, but this process needs to be thought out and planned. What are you trying to achieve in terms of the overall appraisal process?

Further, by thinking about and planning these chats sufficiently, you can ensure that you keep on top of small problems before they become major areas of difficulty. You can also make sure that you are providing regular support and encouragement when appropriate.

To make informal chats work, ensure that you:

❑ *Focus on one or two key points;*
❑ *Involve praise as well as brickbats;*
❑ *Allow the individual to contribute fully;*
❑ *Undertake them regularly.*

Team meetings

> ❝ *Our team meetings take place purely for the sake of having a meeting. They get in the way of our own work and achieve next to nothing except to demotivate the staff.* ❞
> **– Sandy McLaren, research engineer**

"Teams" – how much is written and spoken about their importance? "Team meetings" – how often do you get feedback similar to Sandy's?

Team meetings need to be run properly to get the best from them. If Sandy's complaints ring true with you, it probably isn't because your team members are uninterested or bored, but rather because you are not running the meetings in such a way as to make them constructive and useful.

> **Plan your team meetings well in advance. Circulate an agenda if this would be useful, and use the meeting to discuss how the team is doing and where it is going. Ensure that everyone joins in if they wish to and that minutes are circulated quickly afterwards. Think of the team meeting as another way to appraise your team.**

The key to getting the most from team meetings is thought and planning. If you allow too much of a free-for-all, then the meeting will become unstructured and useless.

A good way to structure your meeting might be as follows:

○ *Review current performance: "How are we doing?"*
○ *Key issues; new initiatives.*
○ *Feedback: preferably positive!*
○ *Objectives: "Where is the team going?"*
○ *Strategy: "What are the **immediate** next steps?"*

By following such a structure, you are making team reviews real and meaningful and letting the whole team know where they stand. This should engender a sense of **collective responsibility**.

❝ *Our new team meetings came as a blessing. There was quite a bit of unavoidable overlap between our areas of responsibility and it was amazing how much duplicated effort we managed to cut out after the meetings were instituted. Even better are the new ideas we now come up with.* ❞
– Val Carpenter, marketing manager

Carry on appraising

You should be in no doubt that maintaining your commitment to an effective appraisal system will deliver enormous benefits to your ability to manage.

On-going appraisal is vital to your success – commit yourself to it NOW.

1. Stop equating appraisals with only the formal systems. Informal chats will probably contribute more to the process than anything else.
2. If you are joining a new team or department, start appraising from day one. It will be far harder to get going if you procrastinate.
3. Good management is about preventing problems and avoiding crises – if you are doing your job properly and have your finger on the pulse of what is happening around you through constant appraisal, you will rarely be involved with crisis management in the future.
4. Review individuals and teams constantly. Make sure you allocate time in your diary for frequent informal ten-minute chats with all of your staff and use team meetings to get a feel for the wider picture.
5. Balance criticism with praise whenever possible. The idea is to inspire, not drain their enthusiasm and confidence.
6. Plan all appraisal activity properly – if you rush it and are ill-prepared you make yourself look stupid and discredit the idea of appraisal.

TIPS

What's in this chapter for you

> *Understanding the paperwork*
> *Getting the timing right*
> *Balanced reviews*
> *Why interviews are vital*
> *Types of formal systems*
> *Get the most from formal appraisals*

> ❝ *My boss was an 'ideas man'. He owned the company so who was I to argue?! He picked up the idea of appraisals from a management book and dreamt up an assessment form which would have driven the Plain English Society to drink. None of us knew how to complete it in a sensible way yet the boss refused to see it as anything other than the work of a genius!* ❞
> **– Dave Taylor, systems analyst**

So far, we have looked at the informal appraisal skills that you as a manager must use daily. It is now time to look in detail at formal appraisal skills and techniques.

Most organisations have formal appraisal systems which involve all members of staff and which are documented carefully. These systems come in all shapes and sizes though typically they would have the following common characteristics:

○ *Documentation*
○ *Defined cycles*
○ *Review*
○ *Interview.*

Let's look at these in more detail.

Documentation

Most systems are ultimately based on a series of forms which have to be filled out. Often the paperwork is structured to follow a logical sequential process.

The paperwork is a means to an end not the end in itself. Do you use paperwork as an appraisal tool or is it something which simply makes your pending tray look like the United Nations building?

In well-established systems, you may well find guidance notes for the appraiser and for the appraisee on the documentation. If they make sense to you, *use them*. If they don't make sense and don't offer genuine help, then *get them changed!*

Understand the paperwork

- ❑ *If you don't understand all of the documentation involved, ask!*
- ❑ *Explain the paperwork to your staff right from the start. If you are seen to not fully understand it, and can't explain it properly, then your commitment to the whole process will be called into question.*
- ❑ *Don't accept everything that is written on the form as sacrosanct. If it needs to be changed, or if you are being asked to use a formal document that is out of date or no longer relevant, get it changed. Using obviously flawed systems will debase the entire process.*

Defined cycles

Most systems have a pre-determined timetable which sets out the number and sequence of appraisals. Commonly they take place annually, with six-monthly updates. You obviously need to understand the timing and sequence of the system that you are expected to use.

Get the timing right

- ❑ *Don't forget, appraisal should be on-going – think of the formal appraisals as milestones which help you through the cycle.*
- ❑ *If you think the formal appraisal takes place too often or too infrequently, argue your case with the powers that be – take ownership of the process.*

Reviews

Most systems incorporate a review by the appraiser of the appraisee. Commonly, this will look at performance (against agreed targets), training and development, and objectives. The system should break the review down into the relevant sections in order that the appraisal is comprehensive. Different systems will do this differently, but you need to ensure that the review is:

○ *objective;*
○ *based on examples of behaviour and approaches, not feelings and impressions;*
○ *balanced (i.e. looks at strengths **and** weaknesses);*
○ *comprehensive, looking at the entire period and not distorted by major or recent incidents.*

Most review systems include some sort of self-review by the appraisee. Make sure that you use this positively. Individuals can be too self-critical – people can be reticent about appearing too self-congratulatory – and your job as the appraiser is to give balanced feedback. Make sure that you give praise and highlight strengths whenever appropriate.

Use self-assessment as a positive method of highlighting good points and building the individual's confidence.

Interviews

Most formal systems culminate in a one-to-one interview between appraiser and appraise. (You will see in chapters 5 and 6 the techniques for conducting the interview effectively.) However, at this stage you need to be aware that very often both the **perceived** and **actual** success of the appraisal as a whole will be determined by the interview.

❝ *In my first managerial role, I had followed all of the various appraisal processes to the letter up until the point of the interview. For some reason, through a misunderstanding, the first one I did ended up in an argument. This totally demoralised both my staff member and myself and ruined the entire process.* ❞
– Lesley Stamp, publisher

Make sure that your staff have an opportunity for a proper and comprehensive interview and give that interview the time and attention it deserves. Remember, appraisal is a two-way process.

Types of Formal System

There are many different types of formal system and often organisations rightly spend an awful lot of time and effort developing one which is unique and which fits their specific needs. However, it is possible to identify three generic types.

1. Freestyle format

This describes a free and fairly unstructured approach. Very often the only guidelines laid down are general headings and the completion of the system involves free-hand notes made by the appraisee and appraiser. These might include such headings as:

- overall performance;
- review of objectives;
- training needs;
- career development.

> **❝** My first appraisal in my current company came as a huge relief. It was very open and fluid and took into account the fact that what I am trying to do at work all day is to be creative. It's a million times better than my old firm, where virtually everything I did had to be justified to the boss. This involved sitting through a torrent of critical remarks from a colour-blind, opinionated idiot. **❞**
> **– Steve Rowe, designer**

Characteristics of freestyle systems are:

- No grading or rating is given and it is the comments and notes which form the basis of the assessment.
- They rely heavily on the appraiser knowing the appraisee well and having sufficient knowledge and skill to make meaningful comments and notes.
- They can be time consuming and over detailed unless managed well.
- They can cover a lot of ground.
- They deal extremely well with qualitative issues.

○ *Unless handled very carefully, they can be subjective and non-specific.*

If you do use this freestyle method of appraisal, make sure that you personalise it to the individual concerned and avoid generalisations or platitudes.

In reality, this system is most suited to appraisers with a small number of staff to appraise, perhaps in a small business where both parties know each other well and have a high level of direct contact.

2. Grading/rating systems

These are very common within most appraisal systems and the principal is to award "marks" to an individual against specific criteria. The key to these systems being used successfully is that the both the criteria against which marks are awarded and what the marks mean are clearly explained and understood by everyone . The more effective of these systems break down the criteria and the ratings into specific, objective and measurable aspects of the job.

If you need to use a grading/rating system, make sure you fully understand how it works and the criteria used. Also make sure you understand how they might apply to an individual in a specific or specialist role.

    " *I find gradings rather difficult to give. If you mark low, it can start an argument; if you go high, it can make them big headed. I tend to play it safe and give lots of middling scores. It seems to work pretty well as everyone seems quite happy about it.* **"**
    – Jill Parks, revenue consultant

Jill's approach is fairly common with these sort of systems. Marking people right in the middle is seen to be safe and uncontroversial. However, it also means that you have to be aware that this method can become bland and meaningless.

> When using grading/rating systems, make sure that you are being fair to your staff. Mark them objectively against the criteria, not against some "safe" norm.

> **"** *I hate our appraisal system. My boss can be really tough and I end up getting a lower grading from her than my friends doing the same jobs in other departments. It's really unfair.* **"**
> **– Jim Wilson, accounts clerk**

Jim's grumble about grading/rating systems is not uncommon. Very often, perceptions arise that certain people are "soft" or "hard" graders. This may indeed be true or it may simply be office gossip. Whichever it is, it can undermine the entire process and as such needs to be dealt with.

> To ensure consistency with grading systems, always try to work to well-defined criteria. Also, meet with other managers and discuss consistency of gradings.

Often ratings/gradings systems have comments boxes at the side in which the grading you give can be explained in some detail. This narrative feature is important as it relates the grading to the individual concerned and makes it personal and specific.

> Where there is a comments box on the appraisal form use it properly. Don't fill it in with non-specific waffle, but use it to support your grading decisions clearly and fairly.

3. Pay-related systems

Performance-related pay became the buzzword of the 1980s and has become widely accepted in a substantial range of businesses.

The mechanism for linking performance with pay quickly became the formal appraisal system. In fact many systems have been developed whereby an overall grading is given which then equates to a percentage pay rise.

> ❝ *I know I'm the best so I wouldn't put up with any sort of appraisal system in which my ability wasn't reflected in my salary cheque. The others could be replaced easily but not a performer like me, and the company's smart to recognise that!* ❞
> **– Keith Gant, advertising sales manager**

Pay-related systems might sound great for some but there are numerous problems with such appraisal methods.

○ **They skew the outcome of the appraisal**
   The appraisees focus on what's in it for them (their potential pay rise) and ignore everything other than the final grading.
○ **The appraisal loses its breadth**
   Such systems encourage a narrow focus on certain performance criteria and often fail to deal with development issues or needs (i.e. training, personal objectives and improvement opportunities).
○ **They commonly overlook individual circumstances**
   Typically, appraisal systems are generic and when pay is linked directly it is difficult to account for differing individual situations (e.g. new starters, job movers, additional responsibilities).
○ **They only focus on individuals**
   Individual contribution is important but, increasingly, team effectiveness is crucial. Singling out individuals can be counter-productive and adversely affect teamworking.

> ❝ *He grabs all of the glory and all of the cash allocated to pay rises. Our appraisal process just doesn't pick up on all the path-breaking work I do on the new accounts – and without it Gant would show up as the useless buffoon he really is. There's no way I can compete with the number of contracts which have his name on the bottom so I always miss out. I'd love to shake up the system or wring Gant's neck – preferably both.* ❞
> **– Ellen Back, Keith Gant's PA**

The message in this book is based on the belief that pay should not be linked to the appraisal system. Have a separate pay review system which takes into account what the company can afford, individual performance, team performance and achievement of objectives.

Move away from individual incentives to team-based incentives. Reward performance and link the term's achievement to pay, but do not allow this to dominate the total appraisal process.

Get the most from formal appraisals

If handled properly, formal appraisals can be exploited as an invaluable supplement to any fully fledged appraisal process.

Look carefully at the tools in your system and think about how to use them realistically.

1. Don't accept formal appraisal paperwork as some kind of sacred script. If it needs to be modified or it's no longer relevant, get it changed. Using flawed systems will debase the entire process.

2. If you do not fully understand the system you've inherited, seek help! If you don't appear confident, in control and committed, the whole process will be undermined.

3. Allow plenty of time to complete the documentation properly. Your appraisees will be expecting a useful outcome if they believe in your commitment.

3. Explain all the processes clearly and make sure everybody understands them.

4. When undertaking reviews, make them comprehensive, balanced, and objective. They should not focus on one-off events or be based on hunches and gossip. Give praise as well as criticism so far as is possible.

5. Be consistent in applying assessment criteria, especially when using gradings/ratings systems. Ensure that everybody fully understands what the benchmarks are.

6. Think of the formal appraisal as a summary which supports, but doesn't replace, your day-to-day management activity.

What's in this chapter for you

Planning for the formal appraisal
Communicating what is involved to all
Scheduling
Getting the information together
Handling the paperwork
Making it personal
Preparing for the interview

When and where?

> ❝ *I can't believe the contrast. My old boss used to appraise me against benchmarks he made up during the formal interview. Because he never used the notes from the previous interview, we never covered the objectives we'd agreed. I began to doubt my sanity. In my new firm, the appraisals are almost totally predictable. My new departmental head covers* **all** *of the issues step by step and truly works with me. I've really developed professionally and I'm so much more confident.* ❞
> **– Karen Butcher, sales representative**

By now you have become a good, caring manager and you're busy all the year round appraising and reviewing your staff. As we saw in the last chapter, nearly every company's appraisal scheme culminates in a formal interview and the success or otherwise of this last key event will make or break the whole process. You must, therefore, ensure you have planned and prepared properly for this interview.

Do not be prepared to undertake any appraisal activity on the spur of the moment. Failing to plan and prepare negates all of your other appraisal activities.

With your commitment to undertaking regular and on-going appraisal, planning should become easier. The planning and preparation for the formal appraisal should begin with the follow-up from the previous informal appraisal – a truly continuous process!

Assume as in most companies that the formal process takes place annually. The following general tips will prove useful to you in dealing with this form of appraisal:

- ○ *Ensure that the personnel department, or whoever centralises the process, keeps you informed of all appraisal commitments.*
- ○ *Book the date in your diary and treat it as an unbreakable obligation.*
- ○ *Be proactive – don't sit and wait for the relevant information to come to you, go and find it yourself and do this well in advance.*

You know it is going to happen, so don't try to put it off. Get organised early on. Remember, successfully completing the process is probably the most important activity you will undertake as a manager!

Personal planning and communication

❝ *I have a team of 15 people and the company system is such that they must be appraised no later than the anniversary of their joining the company. Year one was a disaster. I suddenly got eight appraisal forms hitting my desk from personnel on Friday afternoon with a terse note to say that they needed to be completed by the following Wednesday. It was just impossible.* ❞
– George Archer, senior consultant

It doesn't matter how good you feel your are at handling the informal, day-to-day appraisal elements of management. The formal appraisal is vital in order to close the loop and not being fully aware of your commitments to the process, as in George's case, is a recipe for disaster. Not only does it appear sloppy and disorganised in front of your staff, but it will do you no favours with your own boss when you come to be appraised!

Work backwards from the target completion date and set out the steps needed to complete the process. Write in your diary the deadlines for completing each stage and make sure your schedule allows enough time to do each task comprehensively.

For example, if Chris (yes, him again!) needs to be appraised by July 3rd, your schedule might look something like this:

- ○ **July 3** – *Return completed forms to personnel dept.*
- ○ **July 2** – *Sign completed documentation with Chris.*
- ○ **June 28 to July 1** – *Write-up interview; finalise documentation.*
- ○ **By June 26** – *Appraisal interview.*
- ○ **By June 19** – *Review self-appraisal; complete interview plan.*
- ○ **By June 12** – *Complete written assessment; self-assessment form back from appraisee.*
- ○ **By June 5** – *Hold brief meeting with Chris to explain the appraisal system and hand over self-assessment material.*
- ○ **By June 1** – *Get appraisal documentation from personnel dept and review previous reports; collect and collate necessary information from other sources.*

This will set out the milestones and treats appraisal as a project, the stages of which need to be managed accordingly.

> Approach the formal appraisal as though it were a multi-stage project:
>
> - ❑ *If you are new to appraisals and are unsure of the time sequence involved, take advice from more experienced colleagues.*
> - ❑ *Things always take longer than anticipated. Build in some extra time to your schedule to ensure that unforeseen events don't mess the whole process up.*
> - ❑ *Communicate thoroughly with the people involved and ensure that they know their part in the process. Do this as early as you can to avoid clashing with other commitments such as vital meetings or holidays.*
> - ❑ *If you have several appraisals to do at roughly the same time, don't be tempted to get them all out of the way in one day. To do so will mean that you are not doing justice to everyone involved in the process. Stagger them as widely as you can.*

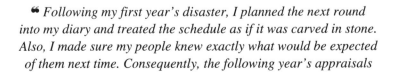

❝ *Following my first year's disaster, I planned the next round into my diary and treated the schedule as if it was carved in stone. Also, I made sure my people knew exactly what would be expected of them next time. Consequently, the following year's appraisals*

went really smoothly. I'm now really happy that I've got the right balance between my informal and formal appraisal skills. **"**
– the enlightened George Archer

Remember: the more that you involve your people in the process, the more likely they will be to want to participate fully. So, communicate with them. Nearer the date of the interview, confirm specific times with them again and double check that they are fully aware what is required of them. This way you will enable the interview to be open and two-way.

" *My first boss caught me one morning at the coffee machine. He asked me to get him a hot chocolate and take it to his office – it was time for my appraisal interview. That was the first I'd heard about it!* **"**
– Ken Castle, bank employee

Ken's boss is not now making a living teaching appraisal skills!

Getting the information together

To prepare for the interview, you will need to collate information about the appraisees. Obviously, this should be taking place as part of your overall commitment to on-going appraisals and should therefore be little more than a summary exercise! However, you may need to gather some information from other sources, such as supervisors or from other departments the appraisee comes into contact with.

> When seeking input from others, avoid subjective, non-specific opinions. Snap judgements are neither valid nor fair and should be dismissed. Get a well-rounded view from as many sources as possible.

Most of the information you will need will have been collected during your on-going informal appraisal activities so you will need to refer to the notes you took . However, ensure that you are referring to the whole period – avoid concentrating on issues confined to just a couple of months or so, as this will distort the total picture.

> Unexpected events (both at work and at home) can cause short-term distortions in the performance of most of us. Use your notes from on-going appraisals to give you a true picture of activity over the **whole** period under review. Avoid, too, being influenced by anything which took place outside of that period.

Documentation

Whatever system of formal appraisal your company uses, there will normally be some associated documentation which will need to be completed prior to an appraisal interview as well as after it. There are myriad forms used by companies, some designed in-house, others bought off the shelf. We are not going to set down for you a hard and fast ruling as to what you should use. Chances are you will have little say in it at this stage anyway! But, as we saw in the last chapter, you must make sure before the interview that both you and your appraisees know how the paperwork is used.

Well in advance of the interview, in addition to checking that you have all of the relevant documentation, you will need to ensure that you have all of the background material necessary to complete the appraisal. This will probably include:

- ○ *All of the recorded personal details;*
- ○ *Up-to-date job description;*
- ○ *Date of commencing employment;*
- ○ *Conclusions from last appraisal;*
- ○ *Previously agreed objectives.*

> What do you think of your documentation relating to the interview?
>
> ❑ *Is it clear enough and easy to use?*
> ❑ *Will it help you achieve what you want to?*
> ❑ *Does it cover everything you need to?*
> ❑ *Is there anything which could be cut out?*

There is a danger that the paperwork can become, or be seen to have become, a bureaucratic nightmare and a paper-chasing exercise. If you feel this is the case with your appraisal documentation, it is probably because of faults in your system. Ask some searching questions:

○ *Is it badly designed?*
○ *Has it been put together without your specific needs in mind?*
○ *Is it well past its sell-by date and not taken seriously by the staff?*
○ *Is it not being properly used or understood?*

The chances are that the problem is a combination of all of these factors, and more.

Documentation should be a means to an end, not the end in itself, and needs to be treated accordingly. Making an assessment of the paperwork you will be expected to use is a vital part of the planning process. Your first responsibility is to fully understand the detail – if you have any queries, get them answered. If you feel changes are crucial, do as much lobbying as you can to have them made.

> **"** *A new manager arranged to see me about the company's formal appraisals. She was having difficulty making the documentation relevant to her team. She pointed out some major flaws and I quickly realised that our system had been designed to cope with the workforce of ten years ago. It hadn't really moved on since then. We ended up designing a completely new system – which works!* **"**
> **– Heather Hartley, personnel director**

If you can't make the documentation work, talk to somebody about it. It might be your problem. If it still doesn't work, try to get the system upgraded. Either way, if you have any queries, get them answered!

Making it Personal

One of the most common problems with written appraisals is that they have a tendency to become bland and repetitive. The same old clichés are trotted out year after year.

❝ It seems inevitable – you end up putting things down like: 'Could do better when it comes to filling in forms', 'She gets on well with her colleagues' or 'He has a good telephone manner'. It's always so bland. I'm really tempted one time to put 'His homework is always late and he should stop talking in class'. I don't reckon anyone would notice! ❞
– Richard Cross, systems analyst

To make the appraisal effective, you need to personalise it and make it specific and relevant (and therefore meaningful!) to the individual.

If you want to make your appraisals effective, make your comments specific and accurate.

- ❑ *Avoid platitudes – people want to know how they are **really** doing.*
- ❑ *Spend time thinking about the person involved. Don't rush it and don't put down the first thing that comes into your head for the sake of it.*
- ❑ *If it starts reading like a school report, stop! You are not there to patronise your staff – make it meaningful!*

Individual interview planning

❝ My manager is very good at filling in the appraisal form and always makes sure that we fill in our individual reviews prior to the interviews. But his interview technique is hopeless! He waffles on and on, constantly trying to find bits of paper to read from, and he won't let me get a word in edgeways. He's mastered the art of talking a lot but not saying anything – I might as well not be there. ❞
– Steve Bates, sales executive

If you get the interview wrong, then all of your good work previously will have been absolutely wasted. The only way to succeed is to plan each individual interview.

When planning the interview, think about the following:

- ☐ **Structure** – develop a simple structure for the interview which will ensure you cover all aspects of the appraisal.
- ☐ **List issues** – identify and list the specific issues that you want to cover in an order that you are comfortable with.
- ☐ **Reactions** – try to anticipate any problems or reactions that the appraisee might bring up.
- ☐ **Outcomes** – Identify the key outcomes you are hoping to achieve.

If you have this kind of blueprint before each formal appraisal, then you can truly focus on the individual concerned and develop a simple plan which will make the appraisal highly specific and relevant to them.

Once you have formulated a plan, stick to it! By doing so, you will manage and control the interview and be totally prepared for all outcomes.

The practicalities

❝ Our company has a very tight and slick appraisal system. All the relevant forms appear as if by magic from personnel; the management and staff are all committed to the process. Then, on the day of the interview you find the only place you can conduct it with a reasonable degree of confidentiality is the broom cupboard or the car park. It is absolutely ridiculous. ❞
– George Jeffries, team leader

You've done all the paperwork, you've spent the last year continuously assessing your staff and the big day for the interview arrives – don't blow it by overlooking the detail!

Make sure that you have thought about and planned both the timing and the location.

Timing

Allow yourself plenty of time to complete each interview properly. Don't stack them up too closely and allow for the unexpected – a major unforeseen problem might arise which needs dealing with immediately and at some length. Also, if you anticipate several potentially difficult interviews, do not arrange them consecutively as it may affect your judgement, attitude and approach (to say nothing of your mental stability!).

Remember: to do justice to your staff and yourself, you need to be as fresh as possible for each interview.

Location

You need somewhere that is private and guarantees confidentiality but which is also comfortable. It is unlikely that an open plan office or the staff canteen will give you enough peace and quiet. If you have your own quiet office then use that if you have exhausted all other possibilities but keep the door shut and transfer all calls during the interview. Arrange the seating so that you are not seen in a dominant position.

If you find it impossible to use your own office, then you may well have to book another room in the building well in advance. Again, if this is likely to be a problem, plan ahead.

Planning to perfection

With careful preparation, you can effectively link your informal daily appraisal activity with the necessary formal appraisal as dictated by your company. Once you have planned for the formal interview, you are ready to close the circle.

Preparation for the formal appraisal is vital.

1. Make sure you schedule all of the necessary steps properly in your diary, including the process of getting hold of all the paperwork and information well in advance.
2. Space out your formal appraisals. Never be tempted to do several appraisals in close succession. You will not be fresh and attentive and will not do justice to yourself or your staff.

3. Ensure you make use of the notes you've been compiling in the on-going appraisal process to plan what you will cover in the formal review. That way you avoid snap judgements or being overly influenced by just recent events.
4. Don't get bogged down in the paperwork. If it is unwieldy and a hindrance to the overall process, do whatever you can to get it changed. You're a manager, not a paper pusher!
5. Appraisal is personal. Avoid clichés and stock phrases and write genuinely about the individual concerned.
6. Get the when and where right. Appropriate planning should allow you to avoid rushing it and ensure the location is conducive to a frank, two-way exchange of views.

What's in this chapter for you

What's the interview meant to achieve?
Setting the right atmosphere
Managing the interview
Controlling the interview
Agreeing outcomes and summaries
Applying communication skills
Where do appraisal interviews go wrong?
The follow-up

❝ *I'd been assessing the individuals in the team on an on-going and continuous basis. I'd checked out the paperwork and covered all the preliminaries such as location and timing. I'd done all of the groundwork – then on the big day I completely blew it!* ❞
– Chris Douglas, marketing director

What's the interview meant to achieve?

The success or otherwise of the whole appraisal process will be dependent upon the interview. Regardless of all of the effort you've put in building up to it, if you don't get it right then the whole thing will have been a waste of time.

Sorry if that sounds a little dramatic, but it is actually true. If you cannot use the appraisal process successfully, it's highly unlikely your career as a manager will amount to much!

Let's remind ourselves of our original definition from chapter 1 (again!).

Appraisal is the on-going, two-way communication process which assesses and reviews

○ *capabilities,*
○ *performance, and*
○ *needs.*

It provides a means of giving and getting **regular** feedback.

Now we are at the interview stage. The key words here are "two-way communication". Remember that the interview is for the benefit of the appraisee and provides you with the opportunity to formally:

○ assess performance,
○ review progress,
○ deal with problems,
○ give praise, and
○ motivate.

"Ah," I hear you say, "what about discipline? Isn't this the perfect time to reprimand the ubiquitous Chris for his slack time keeping, appalling dress sense and dubious personal hygiene?" Well, now you come to mention it . . . IT ISN'T!

If you have been appraising all year then issues of discipline should have been dealt with on an on-going basis, not now at the interview stage.

The appraisal interview should be a positive experience for all concerned. The interview itself should give the opportunity to get the key positive messages across so that the appraisee clearly understands where they stand at present against what is expected and what the future should or could hold for them.

Setting the right atmosphere

It is easy to forget how intimidating some people can find any interview. Often we assume because we know the people being appraised that the appraisal interview will be relaxed and informal and that everyone will be at ease.

> ❝ Even though I'd worked for Gail for months and got on really well with her, when we sat down for my formal appraisal interview I just clammed up and started fidgeting uncontrollably. Poor Gail was thrown completely. It's a good job she's totally committed to on-going appraisal, otherwise my personnel file would portray me as completely unsuitable for my job. ❞
> – Simon Hope, customer service executive

Don't assume people will be comfortable in the interview. An appraisal interview is formal and can be every bit as daunting as being interviewed for a new job. As mentioned in the last chapter, it is important to find the right venue – try to avoid your own office as it is very much your territory. If possible choose somewhere neutral.

When selecting the place for the interview, avoid the following:

❑ *Interviewing across a large desk – it's too intimidating.*
❑ *Using strong lighting – it's an interview, not an interrogation!*
❑ *Symbols of power – don't tower over the interviewee in your luxury executive chair when they are perched below you on a stool.*
❑ *Interruptions – when in the interview, have the courtesy to ensure that you are not interrupted under any circumstances (with the possible exception of the building being on fire, or the imminent arrival of a tidal wave).*

Make sure that the centre of the appraisal is the appraisee.

Managing the interview

It is your responsibility as the appraiser to successfully manage the interview and if you've done all the preparation and planning this job should be much easier for you . Now you just need to ensure that the actual dynamics of the interview are right and that you are in a position to control and manage the interaction. The component elements of the meeting should be as follows:

○ *Opening*
○ *Discussion*
○ *Agreed outcomes*
○ *Summary.*

That's quite easy, isn't it? Let's now look at these individually.

Opening

Expect the appraisee to be nervous, so be aware that you need to put them at their ease.

Always welcome them and thank them for coming. Smile. Explain the purpose, structure and format of the interview and that it is very much a two-way exchange of views. Get your body language right from the start. Don't sit too upright, relax – this will help to assure the appraisee that your interview technique was not learnt from the Chilean secret police.

You need to establish a rapport quickly and break the ice. You can ask general informal questions which allow the appraisee to talk about themselves or their interests a little. These questions might be as simple as:

- ○ *"How are things?"*
- ○ *"How was the holiday?"*
- ○ *"How is the family?"*
- ○ *"How is the job going?"*

If you know your appraisee well and you are both keen on sport, you could say: "I see your team were well beaten on Saturday again!" The point is to make it personal and relaxed.

However, don't let this drag on too long – if the appraisee is too garrulous on the personal front, then firmly but politely ensure that the general conversation is guided back to an explanation of the aims and purposes of the appraisal process. This should then move you seamlessly into the next stage.

Discussion

This must be led by you and should follow the interview plan that you have prepared.

Raise the key points/issues from the appraisal you have done so far and discuss your observations. Draw out and encourage meaningful input.

So, you may ask:

- ○ *"How would you rate yourself with regards to the quality of your work?"* or
- ○ *"How do you feel you work with and fit into the team?"*

Always ask open questions – those that start with "How?", "Why?", "Where?", "When?", etc. By doing so you will draw a response from the appraisee and very often this response will coincide with the issues you wish to raise yourself.

> **❝** *I find that most people are aware of their weaknesses and are self-critical. By asking them the right interview questions, you can make sure that their worries are dealt with in the right context and with a sense of perspective. I try to give the impression that we are 'just having chat' but at the same time I'm directing the discussion to cover the ground I want to cover.* **❞**
> **– Jill Jenkins, HR director**

As the conversation, controlled by you, develops, it is essential that you make summaries at key points and when key issues are agreed upon by both parties. Summarising is an easy way to lead into the next part of the discussion. You can use such phrases as "So you'd agree that your great strength is in supporting the less numerate members of the team?" This in turn might lead you to a discussion of future training needs or a new role within the team.

> **❝** *My boss is excellent at allowing you to actually talk to her in the interview. She seems genuinely interested in my opinions and on the last two occasions has actually said that she has learnt a lot about the company from talking to me!* **❞**
> **– Judie Wilks, customer service supervisor**

Don't be tempted to rush the discussion process on as the appraisee will not feel that the interview is for their benefit at all. Don't watch the clock too much but try to let the discussion run its course.

Try to keep in control of the discussion stage. Neither of you should be dominating the conversation – it should be a balanced exchange of opinions. If you do come up against a waffler of Oympic standard, then ensure you firmly bring the conversation back to what is relevant to both of you. Don't be rude, but by the same token don't allow yourself to sit through an hour long account of their struggle against paper-clip

---

Inevitably within any discussion there will be different perspectives and potential disagreements which could block progress. You need to acknowledge such disagreements and try to work through them. Try to find a middle ground that you both agree on and at all costs avoid the pantomime approach to interviewing – "Oh yes you are!" . . . "Oh no I'm not!"

Agree to disagree if you must and confirm what action you will take in order to move on.

> **Don't get bogged down in disagreements. Very often they can be dealt with better at the end once the whole discussion has taken place and you both can see issues in their full context. Remember, the easiest way to lose control is through disagreement and conflict.**

Within the discussion, learn to take on board and accept points and issues raised by the appraisee. The process is meant to be two-way so you should be prepared to move your position or agree to a change that has been suggested to you. To be seen to be doing this encourages the appraisee to believe in the process and will help to engender commitment to the outcomes and processes.

> **By being seen to be responsive and to be listening to the appraisee, you will help ensure that they feel ownership of the process and that it is truly their appraisal.**

Agreeing outcomes and summaries

The discussion is not simply there to enhance your reputation as company agony aunt or uncle. It should lead to:

○ *Commitment to change and/or improvement;*
○ *Acceptance of personal objectives;*
○ *Training and development commitments;*
○ *Agreed follow-up.*

The skills you should be developing as an appraiser involve using the system and the discussion to achieve agreed outcomes. This can be achieved by:

○ *summarising key aspects and agreeing what the next step should be, and*

○ *seeking ideas from the appraisee on what they think they should do next.*

Decide which method for agreeing outcomes suites both you and the appraisee best.

It is a fundamental requirement that clear and agreed outcomes are achieved as a result of the interview and that these are summarised in a way that is clear both to you and the appraisee. To fail to do so means that the whole process will have been devalued and ultimately will prove meaningless.

Applying communication skills

To make the interview work, you need to ensure that your communication skills are applied properly. In the appraisal interview the key aspects of communicating are:

○ *Questioning*
○ *Listening*
○ *Understanding*
○ *Empathising.*

You need to understand how to use these key skills effectively

Questioning

Wherever possible, ask open questions which will allow and encourage the individual to talk and will draw out information, views and perceptions. Open questions allow the discussion and interview to flow and encourages involvement and participation. Closed questions – those which can be answered "yes" or "no" – lead to stilted and restricted conversation.

Phrase your questions well and have what you wish to ask mapped out before you start (without appearing to be like a bad chat-show host – i.e. entirely lacking in spontaneity).

Be careful: questions which encourage some people to talk can bring forth long-winded replies which avoid or ignore the key points from others. You need to use specific follow-up questions which will help guide the discussion and allows the appraisee to concentrate on the main issues. So, the main question might be "How do you feel you are doing in your new job?" and the more specific follow-up could be "How do you feel you are progressing with the new accounts software?".

The follow-up should still be an open question, but one that allows the appraisee to focus on specific aspects of their job.

Listening

This is the key skill that you must master if you wish communication to be two-way. Sadly, listening skills are rarely developed or practised. Indeed, it often appears that the more senior people become within the managerial hierarchy, the less listening they do!

When listening properly, what you are actually doing is taking on board what is being said and being seen to be doing so. This may sound insultingly obvious, but it is remarkable how many people fail as managers because they have not mastered this seemingly basic skill.

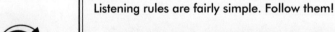

Listening rules are fairly simple. Follow them!

- ❏ *Maintain good eye contact and show that you are interested.*
- ❏ *Verbally and non-verbally acknowledge what is being said.*
- ❏ *Ask relevant questions that relate to what has just been said.*
- ❏ *Paraphrase or summarise at key points in the conversation.*

Understanding

> ❝ When my boss took me through the summary at the end of my interview I was stunned. Either I had been speaking Swahili or he was reading the form from somebody else's appraisal. ❞
> **– Jean Saunders, machine shop supervisor**

You need to ensure that you understand what the appraisee is getting at. This may take some reading between the lines – they may be very nervous or not terribly articulate.

Use some of the following phrases to try to draw out precisely what is meant:

- ❏ *"In other words, what you are saying is . . ."* – this will help to paraphrase what is being said.
- ❏ *"What do you mean when you said . . .?"* – you can clarify difficult concepts so both of you understand what has been said.
- ❏ *"So, pulling all of that together . . ."* – this will enable you to summarise key points.

You also need to ensure that the appraisee has understood you. Check that this is happening by always asking questions when you need to clarify a point and make sure you get a satisfactory response.

Empathising

The ability to put yourself into the shoes of the appraisee is important. By demonstrating that you know what it is like and how it feels, you can break down barriers that might be stopping you from having an open and frank discussion and reach an agreed outcome.

Use such empathetic phrases as:

- ❏ *"I know what it is like dealing with an angry customer on the telephone. When I used to have to take those kind of calls regularly, I found it almost impossible to remember that 'the customer is king'. However, we've got to remember that . . ."*
- ❏ *"I've been in the situation where another supervisor has started yelling and screaming. My first response is to give as good as I get. But that won't really solve anything. We both know we must make sure that . . ."*

By empathising, you let the appraisee know that you are aware of some of the difficulties of their job and that your input is therefore relevant.

Where do appraisal interviews go wrong?

You've seen so far how to conduct interviews to make them as effective as possible. However, even when people have been continuously appraising their staff, and planning and preparing for the final interview, things still can go wrong, thus wrecking the entire process.

Let's look at some of the most common problems at the interview stage.

The talkative appraiser

> ❝ My manager revels in the sound of his own voice. At the interview stage of my appraisal, he talks at length about his problems and about what his priorities are. I rarely get a word in edgeways, and when I do it seems to spur him on to another ten minutes on the onerous responsibilities of being a manger. ❞
> **– Doug Cluny, estate agent**

The appraisal interview should not be about demonstrating how clever you are verbally or unburdening yourself of your own problems. Remember, the process is meant to include two-way communication and is for the benefit of the appraisee.

> Allow the appraisee to talk. Don't try to take over and dominate. You are there to guide and to facilitate.

The monosyllabic appraisee

> ❝ My interview with Jane was very disappointing. I could not seem to get her to talk. She seemed bored by the whole thing and the best I got from her was "yeah" or "no". Talk about pulling teeth! ❞
> **– Karl Rousset, factory manager**

People can be nervous or intimidated by the whole process of being interviewed, as we have said before. Some people are just naturally shy and not used to expressing themselves. It is your job to put them at ease and encourage a two-way discussion.

Remember: most people will relish the chance to talk about themselves. Use the introductory techniques we looked at earlier, starting off with general and open questions. Make it easy for them to participate by finding topics during the early stages that they can speak about and which make them feel involved.

> Be patient in the face of monosyllabic interviewees. Keep trying with open questions and do not allow your frustration to show. It's unlikely that wearing a crazed expression and reaching for their throat will encourage them to be more talkative.

The confrontational appraisee

    ❝ *The interview degenerated into a shouting match and got totally out of control. It all started because I mentioned the quality of Joe's work, merely suggesting that he could speed things up a bit by being more committed to new practices that we were trying to introduce.*
    He took this to be a personal insult and we both just ended up yelling at each other. The stupid thing is that Joe is a good worker and I simply wanted to develop his skills further. ❞
        – Jim Anderson, garage manager

There is often some degree of conflict and disagreement in exchanges between people. However, it is your job to avoid allowing this to develop into confrontation and you should do this by ensuring that you find some common ground as quickly as possible.

> There are some simple rules to help you avoid arguments and conflict.
>
> - ❑ *Don't stoop to personal attacks.*
> - ❑ *Don't use aggressive behaviour.*
> - ❑ *Clarify your point of view with examples.*
> - ❑ *Work back through the key issues if an argument is brewing.*
> - ❑ *Don't get drawn into repetitive arguments (the 'pantomime' syndrome).*
> - ❑ *Agree to disagree, respecting each others opinions.*

If you have tried everything but the argument still seems to be heading inevitably into armed conflict, take a break and allow a cooling off period.

The tangential interviewee

> ❝ *Kathy always goes off in different directions when I do the appraisal interview. I start by discussing her time keeping, she ends up by telling me how much a new carburettor cost her. She has an amazing talent for changing the subject and diverting attention from what I want to talk about.* ❞
> **– Karl Rousset**

As the appraiser, you have to remain in control of the interview and if the appraisee continually digresses then you need to ensure that the issues you want to discuss are returned to. Your interview plan should help with this and you should gently but firmly get the discussion back on track.

> Keep the appraisee from digressing. Try using some 'steering' phrases:
>
> ❑ *"I'd just like to go back to what we said about . . ."*
> ❑ *"I think we've lost the plot a bit here. Let's go on to . . ."*
> ❑ *"Answer the question or I'll sack you . . ."* (no, not really!)

Interviewing is a skill that can be learnt and one that is essential for you to master, not just in the context of appraising but also in the development of your entire management career. So, keep practising and if necessary go on an interview techniques course. But remember: the key to getting it right is in the planning and preparation.

The follow-up

So that's it then. You've done the appraisal interview, signed off on all the paperwork and sent it upstairs or wherever to gather dust. Sure, you are going to be conducting on-going appraisals but essentially you've done your bit.

Wrong! One of the most common reasons why appraisal systems fail is because of the lack of follow-up.

> The follow-up is absolutely vital as it should put into practice the outcomes which have been mutually agreed. Without it, the whole process becomes worthless. Do you fully appreciate the importance of follow-up?

Follow-up needs to be considered as a proactive part of the appraisal process. You will need to consider those issues which demand:

- ○ *Immediate follow-up*
- ○ *Action and support*
- ○ *Reviewing and updating.*

Having followed the appraisal process and reached certain conclusions, you need to strike while the iron is hot. In terms of the formal processes, you need to complete and finalise the post-interview documentation as soon as possible.

> ❝ *I had three consecutive days of appraisals last year and I didn't write up my notes and complete the documentation on each until the end of the following week. When I came to do it I got completely confused! Although, obviously, I'd made individual notes on each person, I ended up being unsure of what had been agreed with whom.* ❞
> **– Ted Foyle, accountant**

Whenever possible, complete the documentation for an individual straight away. Add an hour to your interviewing schedule to ensure that you have time to do this.

Most systems involve some form of final signing off by the appraisee which often takes place a short time after the final appraisal interview. Use this as the first stage of the follow-up. Use the signing off as confirmation of acceptance of the key outcomes and understanding of what is involved. It may only take five minutes but it will reinforce your message and give a very clear indication of your intentions.

As part of your commitment to on-going appraisal, or following the appraisal interview itself, it is vital that you highlight your message and explicitly state your next steps. Let your staff know that you are committed to appraisal and see it as an on-going process.

Immediate follow-up should be allowed for by setting time aside for action which can be taken straight away. There will always be issues that come up within on-going appraisals or from an appraisal interview which can be tackled immediately. So if you decide that a couple of staff members need to improve their knowledge of business finance software, or whatever, arrange for them to attend a course as quickly as possible.

The key to the entire appraisal process is that as a result of it something happens. We have seen how to effectively run the interview and complete the paperwork. Once you have completed the formal interview it's up to you to make sure you follow up on everything you've agreed, and ensure that tomorrow you start the cycle again by resuming your on-going appraising.

Tips on interviews and follow-up

The interview is the culmination of the entire appraisal process and is for the benefit of the appraisee. All of your behaviour should point to this fact.

The more professionally you approach appraisals, the more you will reap from the process.

1. Never use the formal interview for disciplinary action. Deal with such problems as they are happening and ensure that the interview is an uplifting experience.
2. Many people are terrified of interviews. Expect this and ensure that you do everything you can to put the interviewee at ease. Remember also that no two interviews are ever the same. Be prepared for different responses and reactions and keep your head!
3. Compile a list of things you want to cover. This will help you to control the progress of the interview. However, don't script the discussion – let it flow freely in order to achieve a genuine exchange of views.
4. If it looks likely that an argument is brewing, back off and try to cool the atmosphere. Take a break if you need to.

5. Interviewing is an art involving many different skills. Practise these skills or attend a course if needs be – it is very unlikely you will be an effective appraiser unless you are an able interviewer.

6. Write up your interview notes immediately so that they are fresh, personal and relevant. Make sure that the outcomes and objectives are understood clearly by both yourself and the appraisee.

7. If you have agreed to act, make sure you do so and make sure it happens quickly. Failure to do so will undermine not only the appraisal process, but also your credibility as a manager.

8. Don't put your feet up after you've finished the formal appraisal. This is simply the end of one cycle and the start of the next. Your on-going informal appraisal should resume as soon as you've finished signing off the last of the paperwork!

Bon voyage and good managing!

BUSINESS PERFORMANCE + PEOPLE PERFORMANCE
= ORGANISATIONAL SUCCESS

Performance Improvement is a broad-based management consultancy whose aim is to help clients to create the environment for success by focusing on business and people performance. If you would like to hear more or require help with:

- ○ *Process Management and Improvement*
- ○ *Management Training and Development*
- ○ *Human Resource Management*
- ○ *Appraisal Systems and Training*
- ○ *Organisational Change and Development*

Please contact us:

Tel: 0191-428 3403
Fax: 0191-428 3388

Performance Improvement
Suite 103
Tedco Business Centre
Blackett Street
JARROW
Tyne & Wear
NE32 3DT